Aditi and her Friends on their 12th adventure

Beautiful and the Cyberspace Runaway

Aditi and her Friends on their 12th adventure

Beautiful and the Cyberspace Runaway

Suniti Namjoshi

pictures

Proiti Roy

Tulika

Beautiful and the Cyberspace Runaway (English)

ISBN 978-81-8146-781-2

First published in India, 2009
Reprinted 2013

Published by
Tulika Publishers, 24/1 Ganapathy Colony Third Street, Teynampet, Chennai 600 018, India
email tulikabooks@vsnl.com *website* www.tulikabooks.com

Printed and bound at
the ind-com press, 393 Velachery Main Road, Vijaynagar, Velachery, Chennai 600 042, India

For

Vir and Avanti Menon

because I think they'll enjoy it.

THE FOUR ADVENTURERS

Aditi is a brave little girl, who hates fighting, but can wield the Sword of Courage when necessary. She loves the other three adventurers, the two dragons and her grandparents more than anything in the world.

Beautiful Ele the Beautiful Elephant tries hard to be as logical as Siril. Like Goldie she is immensely strong and warm-hearted.

Siril the ant loves maps and long words and his friends. He sometimes wishes he wasn't quite so small.

The One-eyed Monkey or **Monkeyji** is older than the others and so tries hard to be wise and sensible.

THE TWO DRAGONS

Goldie, a fire-breathing sea dragon, and **Opal**, a beautiful and gentle river dragon, fly the adventurers everywhere because they are their friends. They usually live on an island with the Island Sage.

OTHER CHARACTERS

Aditi's grandparents are the rulers of a small kingdom in western India. They have given Aditi and her friends the Sword of Courage, a cloak of invisibility and some magic clay in order to help them protect themselves. The four adventurers live with them.

The Three Sages are three wise sisters for whom the adventurers sometimes run errands. The adventurers can turn to them for help. The Island Sage lives on an island off the west coast of India and is surrounded by lionesses and their cubs. The Marine Sage lives on the Great Barrier Reef off the coast of Australia, and the Techno Sage lives on a lake in Canada.

Little *i* is a runaway computer programme, who has sought refuge with the adventurers. The *i* in her name stands for the square root of minus one, which like her, can be imagined, but cannot exist in the usual way.

1

Beautiful's Decision

A map of the world was spread on the grass and Siril the Ant was walking all over it, stopping first at this location and then at that. Aditi and the One-eyed Monkey were discussing where they might go on their next holiday, and Aditi's grandmother was making suggestions. "Where's Beautiful?" Siril asked. "We ought to consult her."

"I don't know," Monkeyji replied. "She's taken to getting up at four in the morning and taking herself off somewhere."

Just then Beautiful Ele the Beautiful Elephant came stomping across the grass towards them.

"Where do you think we might go on a holiday?" Aditi asked.

Beautiful shook her head impatiently. "I can't go anywhere," she told them. "I have decided."

"You've decided you can't go anywhere?" asked Aditi's grandmother in surprise.

"No, no, I've decided to become rational, sensible, logical, equable — in short, all the things I'm not." She turned to Siril. "You're always telling me I'm too emotional. Well, I'm going to study logic, mathematics and syntax. Then I'll be the most rational elephant in the whole world. Only you all have to help me, please."

"Help you to do what?" asked Aditi.

"Well, you have to help me understand syntax. I was looking over your shoulder yesterday at your exercise book, and saw that the tutor had written: 'Muddled syntax makes for garbled logic.' What did she mean?"

Aditi scratched her head. "I think she meant that the way in which I construct and order my sentences matters. If I say: 'I went for a walk, and I saw Beautiful,' then that means I saw you on my walk. But if I say 'I saw Beautiful and I went for a walk,' then it means that I went for a walk after I saw you."

"Perhaps because I gave you good advice and told you that going for a walk was good for you," put in Beautiful helpfully.

Aditi frowned. "Well, perhaps," she said. She sounded doubtful. "The tutor was saying something about the order implying cause and effect."

"I think I've understood," Beautiful said impetuously. "If I said, 'I baked a cake and I ate it,' then that would be different from saying, 'I ate a cake. And I baked a cake,' wouldn't it?"

"Yes, I think so," Aditi replied hesitantly. "If you just baked a cake and ate it, then that would mean you only had one cake. But if you ate a cake and then baked a cake, you'd have two cakes, wouldn't you? The one you had eaten and the one you had baked?"

"Exactly," agreed Beautiful happily. "The second sort of syntax is much better."

"No, that's not the point. You're supposed to use the right syntax so that you end up saying what you want to say."

"And I say," Beautiful retorted, "that two cakes are better than one. Don't you agree? It's only logical."

At this point Monkeyji intervened.

"What was it you wanted me to help you with?" she asked Beautiful.

"Meditation," Beautiful replied promptly. "You see, I've been getting up very early and going to the Gyaneshwar temple. I fold my legs under me and sit down quietly in front of the statue of Shri Gyaneshwar Maharaj. I sit very still, but my mind isn't still and after a few minutes I start chattering."

"To whom do you chatter?" asked Monkeyji.

"To Shri Gyaneshwar Mowli, of course. Who else? There's nobody else there at that hour." Beautiful looked at Monkeyji in surprise, but when she saw that Monkeyji was looking at her strangely, she decided it might be better not to say very much.

"And does Shri Gyaneshwar Maharaj chat back?" asked Monkeyji.

The truth was that the saint had been talking with her, but she didn't know for sure whether that was her imagination or not. Best not to say anything, she decided.

"Sant Gyaneshwar Maharaj died more than eight hundred years ago, didn't he?" Beautiful replied. "It's just that I like to meditate in front of his statue. Could you help me, please?"

"Of course, I'll help you. It's just a matter of practice," Monkeyji replied.

"And I'd like to help as well," Siril put in. "But I don't know what would be useful."

"Could you help me to understand how to get from Place A to Place B. That's an exercise in logic. I'm always getting lost."

"That's should be quite easy," Siril told her. "It's just a matter of getting your bearings and understanding which way is north."

"But I know which way is north!" exclaimed Beautiful. "It's the way my trunk is pointing and the direction in which I'm looking. I'm clear about that."

Siril sighed. "No wonder you get lost. You're very subjective. Try to be a bit more objective."

"What does that mean?" Beautiful was frowning and beginning to look annoyed.

Siril hesitated. "It means — it means not just looking at things from your own point of view, but looking at things as they really are."

Beautiful glared at him. "So if I say that that way is north, and five or six people say that the other way is north, then I'm just subjective, but they're all objective? Huh! I don't think that's logical at all. They could be wrong."

"You're right," agreed Siril patiently. "So what's needed is external verification."

"What's that?" Beautiful demanded.

"A test," Siril replied, "to establish whether a notion is right or not. For example, if you thought this way was north and I thought that way was north, and we put it to the test, then whichever one of us got to the Gyaneshwar temple first would have been right about their assumption."

"But one of my steps is equal to a thousand of your steps," Beautiful pointed out.

"Well, yes, there's that," Siril agreed. He sounded defeated. "Look, which way is north isn't worth fighting about. It's just a definition. Say you're standing on the surface of the earth – "

"I am," agreed Beautiful. "That's what I'm doing."

"Well, then if you pointed your trunk towards the North Pole, that would be north."

"How would I know where the North Pole was?" Beautiful asked. "After all, it's quite far away, and I've never been there."

"That's a perfectly reasonable question," Siril replied. "In the daytime you can get your bearings from the sun, and at night from the pole star. And if neither the sun, nor the pole star is available, then use a compass. Have you understood?"

"Yes," said Beautiful meekly. "I have to find the North Pole first and then point my trunk, not point my trunk first and then find the North Pole."

"That is, of course, if you wanted to go north. Having found out which way the North Pole is, if what you really wanted was to go south, what would you do?"

Beautiful looked at them. "I would turn around," she said sweetly and smiled at them. It was then that the others realized that she had, in part, at least, been teasing them.

"Well, now that you've had your game, what about looking at the map, and helping us to decide where we might go?" Siril said.

"No, seriously, Siril," Beautiful replied. "I do want to become a rational elephant. What you told me was quite helpful. I do get lost. I don't want to go on holiday. You see, I don't want to be thought of as a silly elephant with no brains at all. I want to stay here and study something difficult."

"Like what?" asked Monkeyji.

"Well, like mathematics," mumbled Beautiful shyly.

"I could teach you some mathematics," offered Aditi's grandmother. "Not a great deal, but some. I've always liked it."

"Something nice?" asked Beautiful hesitantly. She was a little afraid of mathematics.

"I think so," replied the queen. "What about conic sections."

"What does that involve?" Beautiful wanted to know.

"Ice cream," replied Aditi's grandmother without hesitation. "Meet me under the banyan trees at four o'clock."

The others pricked up their ears.

"May we come too?" Aditi asked. "I mean, just to watch."

Aditi's grandmother looked at Beautiful, and Beautiful nodded. Monkeyji, Aditi and Siril looked at each other. Was it possible that learning to be rational was more fun than going on a holiday? Beautiful said nothing at all, but she was feeling extremely pleased with herself. She was sure that very soon she would turn into a very superior elephant.

2

Conic Sections

When Beautiful arrived at the banyan trees, she found that a long table had been set out, and on the table there were a dozen ice cream cones, two or three plates, a gleaming knife and a large dish of pistachio ice cream (Beautiful's favourite). Aditi, Monkeyji and Siril had also got there for four o' clock. They were standing respectfully to one side while the queen gave Beautiful her first lesson in conic sections.

The queen held up an ice cream cone, and handed Beautiful the knife, which Beautiful held by the handle in her trunk. "Slice the extra ice cream off the top of the cone and put it on a plate," the queen instructed Beautiful.

Beautiful did as she was told and then asked politely whether she might eat the extra ice cream, and when she was given permission to do so she licked it up in one scoop. "What next?" she asked.

"Now slice about half an inch off the cone parallel to the top surface," the queen told her.

"May I give the sliced off bit to Aditi?" Beautiful asked.

"Yes," replied the queen, "and when you have done so, look at the cone. What you have on top is a conic section. In this case a perfect circle."

"I see," said Beautiful enthusiastically, "conic sections are sections of ice cream cones."

"Of any cones," the queen corrected. "Now slice the cone at a slight angle. And yes, you can put the top bit on a plate and give it to Monkeyji."

"What's this shape called?" Beautiful asked staring at the top of what was left of the cone.

"That," the queen told her, "is called an ellipse."

"There's very little left of the cone," Beautiful said. "Shall I give it to Siril and we can start on another cone?"

"Do," agreed Aditi's grandmother, and picked up another ice cream cone.

"Who invented conic sections?" Beautiful asked.

"A philosopher called Descartes," the queen told her. "Like you, he believed in being rational."

"And like me, perhaps he liked ice cream," Beautiful added.

While Beautiful went on with her lesson and learned about parabolas, hyperbolas and pairs of straight lines, Aditi, Monkeyji and Siril huddled together and ate their ice cream.

"What are we going to do about Beautiful?" Siril said. "She seems bent on becoming rational."

"I don't want to go on a holiday without her," Aditi put in.

"But if we say we're going on a holiday, I don't think she'll come," Monkeyji murmured.

"Perhaps we should learn mathematics with her," Siril suggested.

"And meditation as well," Monkeyji offered.

"Perhaps," Aditi agreed. "But wouldn't it be good if we could have a holiday and learn these things?"

As she said this they heard the sweep of wings overhead, and in a few seconds the two dragons, Goldie and Opal, had landed on the lawn.

"Hello Goldie! Hello Opal!" Aditi, Siril and Monkeyji called out and ran to greet them. Beautiful, of course, had to stay where she was. She was still learning about conic sections.

"The Island Sage wants us to go to Pune and bring back an acquaintance of hers called Shri Vidvanji," Goldie told them.

"Is he also a sage?" asked Aditi.

"No, he's a mathematician; he likes computers," Goldie replied.

"He's invented something that he wants the Island Sage to try out," Opal put in. "He says it's a thing that everyone in the world should have; but he wants to test it first in case there are snags."

"What is it?" asked Siril.

"I don't know," replied Opal. "If you were to come with us, you could find out."

"Love to," replied Siril immediately.

"Me too," Aditi and Monkeyji said simultaneously.

By this time Beautiful's lesson was over, and the dragons had come up to Aditi's grandmother to pay their respects. Aditi and the others were asking her permission to go with the dragons. Beautiful was tempted to join them. After all, Pune wasn't very far; but she decided that it all sounded too much like a holiday and that what she ought to be doing was studying hard. She said nothing at all.

Goldie noticed this, but he ignored it and said to the others, "Glad you're coming. You see, he lives in the heart of the city, and that's so crowded that we don't think we could land anywhere near his house. We thought we could land on the outskirts of Pune, say on the hillside at Katraj Ghat, and you could go into the city and bring him to us."

"The only thing is it will be quite a long walk," Opal murmured without looking at Beautiful.

"We don't mind," Monkeyji said stoutly. "Siril will ride on my shoulder as usual. And Aditi and I can walk quite fast. I hope, I just hope that Shri Vidvanji doesn't mind walking."

Beautiful began to feel more and more uncomfortable. Surely being rational and studious didn't mean that she couldn't help her friends? "Please," she said to Goldie and Opal. "Can I come too? Then Aditi and Monkeyji and Siril could ride on my back, and on the way back I could carry Shri Vidvanji as well."

Goldie beamed. "That would make a big difference," he told her.

And Aditi gave Beautiful a big hug and said, "I was waiting for you to say you'd come. Things aren't as much fun without you, you know."

And this made Beautiful feel so good that she began wondering whether helping one's friends wasn't at least as important as being rational. "It is," the queen murmured in her ear, reading her thoughts.

"We'll be back in no time," Aditi told her grandmother as they climbed into the howdah on Goldie's back.

"The flight to Pune should only take fifteen or twenty minutes," Goldie said, "though fetching Shri Vidvanji from the middle of the city might take longer."

They waved goodbye and the two dragons rose into the air.

3

Being Sensible Is Sensible, Isn't It?

The flight to Pune was brief and uneventful. They landed on Katraj Ghat and looked down at the city. They would have to walk ten to fifteen miles to get to the old city. Meanwhile they could see cars climbing up the hill like beetles, and heavily laden lorries teetering around the hairpin bends. Beautiful didn't really fancy walking through that sort of traffic and nor did the others. It didn't look safe. And then there was the problem of the petrol fumes. They had all started coughing, and even the dragons had to clear their throats.

Beautiful stared at the scene thoughtfully. "I think this is a problem in what they call logistics, if not in logic. I think we should go home, email Shri Vidvanji that we'll come to fetch him tonight at 2:00 a.m. exactly and that he should be ready. And then at about 1:30 in the morning Goldie and I should make ourselves small, fly to his house in the heart of the old city, land in the street and bring him back quickly."

The others thought about it. "It sounds like a good plan," Siril admitted. "But why should you be the only one to go with Goldie?"

"Because," replied Beautiful, "it's irrational for all of us to stay awake, when it's necessary for only one of us to stay awake."

"That's right," agreed Goldie. "All that's necessary is for me to make myself small, stay awake till the right time and go and fetch Shri Vidvanji."

"But I want to go with you," Beautiful blurted out before she could stop herself.

"Yes, me too. Me too," Aditi and Monkeyji and Siril cried.

"What? Even though it isn't rational?" Opal teased.

"I was thinking," Beautiful muttered tentatively, "that though it's good to be rational, it's not necessarily good to be rational all the time. What do you think?"

"I think you're right. I think the Island Sage would agree with you. But why don't you ask Shri Vidvanji when we fetch him tonight. He's supposed to be a supreme rationalist," Goldie told her.

Nobody wanted to discuss the matter further. Goldie and Opal took off quickly and in no time at all they were back under the banyans. They explained their plan to Aditi's grandmother, had their dinner and then tried to catch some sleep so that they'd be wide awake when it was time to make themselves small and fly to Shri Vidvanji's house. Aditi set the alarm for one-fifteen and fell asleep. It seemed to her that she had hardly slept at all when the alarm went off. She woke up the others.

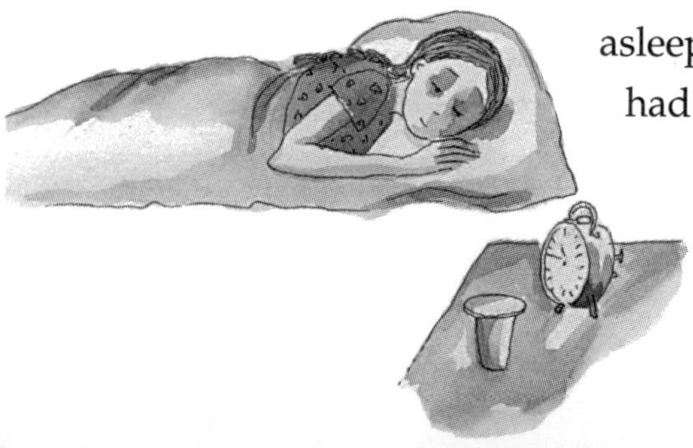

Goldie and Opal were already awake and had begun rubbing the Grow-Small ointment on themselves. They were planning to reduce themselves to Beautiful's size.

"What about me? What size should I be?" Beautiful asked.

Opal considered. "I think you should be about Monkeyji's size. Monkeyji and Siril shouldn't bother to change their size, and Aditi should reduce herself to about half her size so that she's also Monkeyji's size."

This was done quickly enough, but then they had a problem. The howdah was now too large for Goldie to carry. They would have to leave it behind. It was easy enough for Aditi to cling to Goldie's back and for Monkeyji to hang on to Opal while Siril sat on her shoulder, but how was Beautiful to manage?

"We could try tying you on," Siril said doubtfully, "but I don't think it will be safe."

Poor Beautiful was disappointed. She had been looking forward to flying through the night while the rest of the world was fast asleep. She was about to protest, but she remembered that she was trying to be a calm, rational, sensible elephant. She pulled herself together and said, "You don't really need me to come with you if you're going to land outside Shri Vidvanji's house. The sensible thing to do would be for me to stay behind."

"I'm afraid that's true," Goldie told her regretfully. "Never mind. We'll be back soon."

Beautiful waved goodbye to them and looked around. She was wide awake. She decided she might as well go to the

Gyaneshwar temple now instead of going at her usual time at four o' clock in the morning. She trotted along sniffing the night air and looking up at the stars. In five minutes she was there.

There was nobody around. She knelt down in front of the statue of Shri Gyaneshwar Maharaj, closed her eyes and tried to meditate, but her mind was restless. After a while she opened her eyes and said to Shri Gyaneshwar Mowli, "I've been learning about conic sections, you know."

"What are they?" asked the saint.

"Slices of ice cream," she told the saint. "Well, actually the shapes you can make if you slice an ice cream cone."

"I see," replied the saint.

"It's good, isn't it?" Beautiful asked anxiously. "It shows that I'm trying to be rational and all that."

"I don't know," replied the saint.

"Is being saintly the same as being rational?" asked Beautiful. For a moment she thought that perhaps Shri Gyan

Mowli might not know what being rational meant.

"No," replied the saint.

Beautiful shut her eyes again and tried to meditate. After a while she opened them and asked, "Do you think I could ever be a saint?"

"Do you want to be a saint?" Shri Gyaneshwar Maharaj asked.

"I don't think so," Beautiful replied doubtfully.

"Ah well, there's your answer," the saint told her.

For a while the two meditated together. Then Beautiful opened her eyes again. "I was rational at least twice today. The first time I worked out the best way to fetch Shri Vidvanji, and the second time I didn't go because that was the sensible thing to do."

"What would have happened if you had gone?" asked the saint.

"I would probably have fallen off Goldie's back," Beautiful told him.

"Then it's just as well you didn't go," the saint smiled.

Beautiful frowned. "Being sensible is sensible, isn't it?"

"Yes," agreed the saint

Then Beautiful bowed her head and to rose to go.

"I'll come again, probably day after tomorrow morning," she told him.

"Do," the saint replied.

4

Mistress *i*

Beautiful walked back slowly. She always felt better after talking with Gyan Mowli. She wondered whether he had ever walked along this dusty road eight hundred years ago. And if he had, could he have guessed that one day there would be a temple in his honour here and a statue of him? As she was walking along, thinking of this and that, she thought she felt something settle just behind her right ear, something so light that she wasn't sure it was anything at all. She lifted her trunk to check, but a tiny voice cried out, "Oh please don't dislodge me. I'm Mistress *i*. I've taken refuge behind your right ear. Oh please, please, please help me."

The little voice sounded so distressed that Beautiful replied before she could ask herself whether she was being rational, "Of course, I'll help you, little one. What is the matter?"

"You'll soon find out," Mistress *i* replied. "You see, I've escaped. And Shri Vidvanji is making a big fuss. You won't give me up to them, will you?"

Beautiful didn't know what to say. She had promised the little creature, whoever she was, that she would help her; but it would have been more sensible to find out a little more first. "I promise I won't give you up without finding out a little more first."

"All right," Mistress *i* agreed. "But at least don't give away my hiding place for the time being."

"I won't," promised Beautiful. She had a feeling that she hadn't behaved like an entirely rational elephant allowing a little creature she couldn't even see and who had clearly got herself into some sort of trouble to hide behind her right ear, but there was no help for it now. A promise was a promise.

When she got back, she found that all the lights had been switched on and there was a great uproar going on. Everyone was rushing about turning over stones, peering into the trees, even checking the flowers beds. In the middle of it all a tiny man with white hair and green eyes was shrieking at the top of his voice, "Oh she's run away! She's run away! The naughty little thing has run away! And now I'll have nothing to show the Island Sage!"

Eventually, Aditi's grandparents calmed him down. It turned out that he had invented a little Personal Pocket Companion, a thing that was to be part friend, part pet and part computer. It would bond with a particular individual and then be with them for life. He said that he had started out trying to make a tiny computer programme that was exceedingly clever and powerful, but that somehow the thing

had acquired a personality of its own. One day the little programme had told him that her name was Mistress *i* and that she was not bonding with him. She wanted a better friend. He knew there was going to be trouble, so he had asked to see the Island Sage in the hope that she could tell him what he ought to do. But when they had landed on the grass, and he had opened the little computer in which Mistress *i* lived, he realised that she had escaped. She had never done that before.

"Well, never mind," Aditi's grandmother consoled him. "We'll look for her again tomorrow. Perhaps she'll return of her own accord. Try to get some sleep."

"And anyway," Aditi's grandfather said, "now that you've done it once, you can always build another PPC."

"I don't think I can," moaned Shri Vidvanji. "You see, I just set out to build a very tiny, very powerful computer. I think Mistress *i* was an accident. I don't know how she happened."

"Can you find out?" asked Aditi's grandfather.

"Perhaps," replied Shri Vidvanji, "but I'll have to catch Mistress *i* first and cut her open in order to find out."

Beautiful had been listening to all this quietly, and up to this point she had been feeling very guilty. After all, there she was hiding the culprit when everyone else was scurrying about looking for her. But when Shri Vidvanji started talking about cutting up Little *i*, Beautiful stopped feeling guilty at once. She didn't think anyone should be cut up, no matter what they had done. And as for poor *i*, all she had done apparently was run away. Perhaps she had a good reason? Beautiful made up her mind. "Come on," she whispered to Mistress *i*, "Let's get out of here."

"Whew!" Mistress *i* whispered back. "Thanks for not giving me away."

Beautiful slipped away quietly without saying a word to anyone and made her way to the hangar that had been built for her. "Now," she said to Mistress *i*, "I don't know who you are or what you are, but let's get some sleep and worry about what we're going to do with you later."

"Excellent," replied Mistress *i*, "I'm very tired," and settled herself behind Beautiful's ear.

Just before falling asleep herself, Beautiful found herself thinking, 'Here I am, hiding a runaway behind my ear. Am I a sane, sensible, rational elephant?' She feared that the answer was clearly 'No', but that didn't prevent her from falling asleep and dreaming about her new companion. In her dream Mistress *i* was telling her that she knew the answer to everything in the world. At least she thought she was dreaming. "That's absurd," she mumbled sleepily, "how can anyone know all the answers?"

"But I do know them," Mistress *i* replied. "That's how I've been programmed. Go on, test me."

"All right, what's my name?" Beautiful muttered.

"Don't you even know your own name?" Mistress *i* teased.

"All right, I'll tell you. You're Beautiful Ele the Beautiful Elephant and you're the sweetest and most good-natured elephant in the world."

"That's an excellent answer," Beautiful admitted. "What about being the most rational elephant in the whole world? Am I that yet?"

"No," Mistress *i* admitted. "But being rational isn't everything, you know."

"My friend Siril thinks it is," Beautiful replied.

"No, he doesn't," Mistress *i* told her.

"How do you know?"

"I know everything," Mistress *i* replied smugly.

"You're an irritating little thing, aren't you? Now be quiet before I zap you," Beautiful growled.

"You can't zap me," Mistress *i* retorted.

"Why not?"

"Because I'm too little." Mistress *i* sounded pleased with herself. She had clearly won that round.

After that they both fell asleep, and slept soundly till the daylight streaming through the hangar's skylights woke them.

5

Theft or Kidnapping

As Beautiful was waking up slowly she found herself thinking, "There's something I'm going to have to deal with today. What is it?" And then she remembered.

"Come on, Little *i*," she called out. "It's time to show yourself. We've got to have a little talk and decide what's to be done with you."

Little *i* seemed to be able to move with the speed of thought. Before Beautiful had finished speaking she was standing on the ground in front of Beautiful. She was a tiny little thing about half an inch high, and seemed to be made of some flickering opaque substance. Beautiful found herself thinking, "She has the face of a pixie and the manners, the manners ? – the manners of a brat."

"Why does something have to be done with me?" Little *i* demanded. "I'm perfectly happy here."

"But you've run away," Beautiful pointed out.

"When you walk about wherever you like, people don't say you've run away," Little *i* retorted.

"Shri Vidvanji is looking for you. He says you belong to him," Beautiful murmured. She had realised that dealing with Little *i* wasn't going to be easy.

"I'm not a piece of property." Little *i* said indignantly. "I don't belong to anybody."

"She has a point, you know," Siril put in suddenly.

Both Beautiful and Little *i* were startled. "Where did you come from?" Beautiful asked.

Siril shrugged. "I crept in under the door," he said. "I came to wake you and to tell you that Shri Vidvanji has been making a frightful fuss all morning. He says that he's going to see to it that whoever has kidnapped Mistress *i* is severely punished. He says she's worth a king's ransom in gold. In fact, he says, she's probably worth the ransom of a hundred kings. He's gone back to Pune to see if Mistress *i* is lurking in his house." Siril paused.

"I thought you sneaked away in rather a hurry last night.," he said to Beautiful. Then he turned to Little *i* and said, "Mistress *i*, I presume? I am Siril."

Little *i* looked at Siril and was charmed. "Oh," she cried, "you're even littler than me. Let's be friends."

"Thank you," Siril replied, "but you can't just decide to be friends with someone, you know. Friendship has to be worked at."

"Fine," Little *i* replied. "Let's work at it. Where do we begin?"

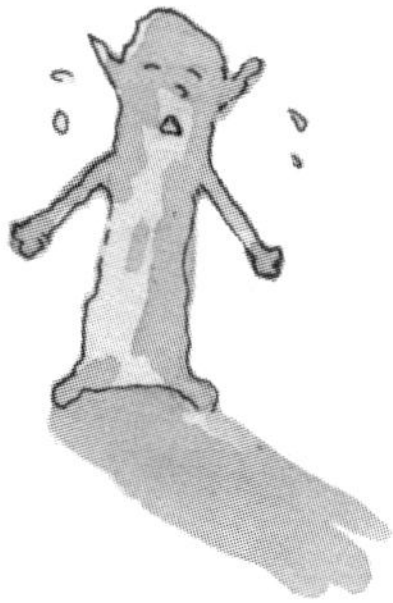

"And it's built up slowly over time," Siril added.

"That's all right," Little *i* told him. "Beautiful's your friend, isn't she?" And when Siril nodded, she went on to say, "Well, then there's no problem. We'll have lots of time. I intend to live behind Beautiful's right ear."

"Hold on!" Beautiful cried. She was startled. "When did I say you could live behind my right ear? In fact, you definitely can't live behind my right ear. It's ticklish."

"Well, your left ear then?" asked Little *i* hopefully.

"No!" Beautiful expostulated.

At this point, to Beautiful's horror and Siril's distress, Mistress *i* began to cry. For such a little thing she cried very loudly. "The fact is," she said in between sobs, "you don't like me very much. And that's not fair. It's not reasonable of you not to like me. I'm very likeable, you know. You're just being mean to me."

While Beautiful and Siril stared at Mistress *i*, who by now was crying at the top of her voice, the door of the hangar opened and Aditi, Monkeyji, Goldie and Opal looked in upon the scene.

"Oh no!" Monkeyji cried looking at Beautiful and Siril in consternation. "Don't tell me you've kidnapped Shri Vidvanji's PPC! Before going back to Pune he made us put up posters everywhere."

Little *i* stopped crying at once. She turned to Monkeyji and said indignantly, "I am not Shri Vidvanji's PPC! I'm nobody's

Personal Pocket Companion. I'm Mistress *i*, if you please! And I was just trying to make friends with Siril here, but it's going to be difficult because Beautiful won't let me live behind her right ear!"

"I see," Monkeyji said quietly. She and Aditi entered the hangar.

The four adventurers sat in a circle around Mistress *i* while the two dragons hovered in the background.

Aditi looked at Little *i* thoughtfully. What were they going to do with her?

"The question is, are you a piece of property or a person?" muttered Beautiful.

"I've told you several times that I'm not a piece of property," Mistress *i* told her. "And anyway if I'm property, then you're a thief!" she added crossly.

"What? But that's rubbish. I didn't steal you." Beautiful was indignant.

"Are you suggesting that a piece of property stole itself? Huh!" Little *i* said scornfully. Then she said in a more ordinary voice, "It's no good arguing with me, you know. I'm a trained computer."

"I thought you said you were a person?" Siril put in.

"So what?" she said to him in a superior fashion. "A does not exclude B. You're an ant. And you're my friend, well, almost my friend. The two categories are not mutually exclusive, you know."

Beautiful stared at her. "Wow!" she said. "What a logician! When Shri Vidvanji finds out that we've got you and charges us with either theft or kidnapping, I hope you'll be able to argue us out of prison!"

Just then Aditi's grandparents entered the hangar.

"I'm afraid that's exactly what you might have to do," Aditi's grandfather said gravely. "Shri Vidvanji has had a warrant issued for your arrest."

"Are we all going to be arrested?" asked Monkeyji.

"Well, he's put down everyone who went to fetch him from Pune, that includes Goldie and Opal. But he left out Siril because he didn't see him. And he has left out Beautiful because she didn't go with you," Aditi's grandmother told them.

"And me," piped up Mistress *i*. "He hasn't put my name down on the warrant."

"Don't worry," she added turning to Monkeyji, "I'll think

of an argument that will get you out of prison in no time at all."

"Don't be silly," Siril said to Mistress *i*, "as soon Shri Vidvanji catches you, he'll put you into the PPC."

"And that really will be prison," Little *i* wailed. She started crying again, but she was crying softly this time, and this was worse than her crying loudly. The poor little thing looked as though she had given up.

In between her sobs she said to the adventurers, "I'd rather go to prison with you than be locked up in Vidvanji's PPC. At least I'd be with friends then, well, almost friends."

"This whole thing is absurd!" Beautiful burst out. "If anyone's going to prison, it should be me. The others didn't even know about Little *i*."

"Did you actually steal or kidnap Mistress *i*," Aditi's grandmother asked.

"No, she didn't. She didn't even know I was hiding behind her ear," Mistress *i* told the queen. "All she did was not give me away when Vidvanji started looking for me. Would you have given me away if I had asked you for sanctuary?"

The king and queen looked down at the little creature at their feet.

"No, we wouldn't have," they said simultaneously.

Then the king added, "Vidvanji is on his way here with the police. I can hold them off by saying that they have no jurisdiction within this kingdom. I'll go to the border and try to stall them. Meanwhile, though, try to think of a plan. I don't think they'll just give up and go away."

It was agreed that the queen and the others would have a quick breakfast and meet under the banyan in half an hour. Little *i* wanted to stay with Siril, and he very generously said she could share his matchbox until the crisis was over. Aditi took the matchbox out of her pocket and put them both inside. Then she and her grandmother and Monkeyji and the two dragons started towards the banyan. Beautiful said she would join them shortly. She ran as fast as she could to the Gyaneshwar temple.

6

A Soul or a Virus?

There were people about at the Gyaneshwar temple, so after she had settled herself in front of the statue of the saint, Beautiful thought at him furiously rather than talking aloud to him.

"I'm in a mess," Beautiful told the saint. "Do you think I should go to prison?"

"I can't see the point," the saint replied.

"But I can't let the others go to prison!"

"That's true," the saint agreed, "but your going to prison isn't going to help."

"What should I do?" Beautiful wailed. "We're in a terrible situation and we didn't even do anything."

"You know what you should do," the saint told her.

"What's that?" Beautiful asked.

"Breathe in and out. Calm down. Make your mind as clear as possible. And then deal with whatever you have to deal with," the saint told her.

Suddenly Beautiful felt better. She meditated for a few minutes, took her leave of the saint and went back to join the others.

"I think what we have to do is join Aditi's grandfather at the border and explain to the police accompanying Vidvanji that no crime has been committed," Beautiful said to the others.

"Are we clever enough to do that?" said Aditi doubtfully.

"And even if we tried," put in Goldie, "they would probably arrest us before we opened our mouths."

"No, I'll do the talking," Beautiful told him. "I'm not very clever, but you see, I'll have Little *i* in my right ear and Siril in my left ear. They'll coach me. And, in addition, Aditi and Monkeyji will be sitting on my back with the cloak of invisibility wrapped around them so they can help me too. As for you and Opal, I doubt very much that they'll be eager to arrest you. After all, where would they put you? What prison would be large enough? They might even be glad to have a reason for not arresting you."

"Wow!" cried *i*. She was perched on the matchbox with Siril. "You'll have six PPC's assisting you. You can't lose."

"They're not PPC's," Beautiful told her. "They're my friends."

"Exactly!" cried Little *i*. "Who'd want a PPC or even want to be a PPC, when they could have a friend or be a friend? Now do you see why I escaped?"

Beautiful looked down at the little creature. She had been a lot of trouble, but Beautiful could see she had a point. "Yes, Little *i*, I do see," she said quietly.

Without further delay, the four adventurers and Little *i* climbed into the howdah on Goldie's back, waved to Aditi's grandmother and took off for the border.

"If we do go to jail," Monkeyji murmured to Beautiful, "Will you come and visit us?"

"What? Don't even think about it. No one's going to arrest you," Beautiful declared.

"But what if they do?" Aditi persisted.

"If they try to do that," Beautiful said, and it was clear she meant it, "I'll just pick them up and throw them into the river."

"But that wouldn't be rational," Aditi pointed out.

"Or even sensible," Monkeyji added.

"And definitely not law-abiding," Siril put in.

When she saw that the others were teasing her, Beautiful grinned. "It won't come to that. You'll see. Not with Mistress *i* and the rest of you to help me."

Within a few minutes the two dragons landed by the river which formed part of the boundary with the district of Pune. On the bridge they could see that Aditi's grandfather was engaged in a fierce argument with Shri Vidvanji, while the District Superintendent of Police stood there and tried to listen to both of them simultaneously.

Little *i* and Siril were already settled in Beautiful's ears. Aditi and Monkeyji had wrapped the cloak of invisibility around themselves and were seated on Beautiful's back. Beautiful climbed out of the howdah and marched up the bridge. The dragons kept their distance.

As Beautiful approached, Aditi's grandfather was just leaving. She heard the District Superintendent of Police say to him, "I'll review the matter of jurisdiction, Sir; but I do have a warrant to arrest your granddaughter and several of her friends, and should I see them, it will be my duty to arrest them."

"Arrest them for what?" asked Beautiful.

"For theft of a PPC from Shri Vidvanji while pretending to transport him and his PPC to the Island Sage," replied the DSP. "I see two of the accused in the distance and will endeavour to arrest them." The DSP pointed at Goldie and Opal.

"What will you do with them?" asked Beautiful. "They're too large to put in prison."

"I will have large chains forged for them and shackle them," the DSP replied.

"Ask him if he'd do that even if they were not guilty," Siril whispered.

"Even if they are not guilty?" Beautiful asked.

"In that case," the DSP responded, "I certainly would not arrest them. I would arrest Shri Vidvanji instead for making false allegations."

This made Vidvanji think again. He knew that sooner or later Opal and Goldie would be able to prove that they really had been sent by the Island Sage. He decided to withdraw his charge against them.

"Well, I take back what I said against the two dragons. Perhaps they really were sent by the Island Sage. Perhaps they had nothing to do with the theft of my property," Vidvanji said hastily.

"Ask him if he's sure his property has been stolen. Tell him he's a learned and absentminded person, and perhaps his PPC is still in his pocket," Little *i* whispered to Beautiful.

"Sir," Beautiful said to the DSP, "Shri Vidvanji has charged

Aditi and Monkeyji with the theft of his property, but what if it should turn out that his property hasn't been stolen at all?"

"Why, I'll put him in prison for wasting police time," the DSP said at once.

"Well," Beautiful said, "Shri Vidvanji is an extremely learned and absentminded person. Perhaps his PPC is still in his pocket."

"Is the PPC in your pocket, Sir?" the DSP demanded sternly.

Vidvanji didn't know what to do. The computer was, of course, still in his pocket and he didn't want to deny it in case the DSP decided to search him. He produced the PPC.

"If you've still got your PPC, why have you been making false accusations?" the DSP thundered at him.

"Oh, I'm not making any accusations at all. In fact, I withdraw my charges against the king's granddaughter and Shri Monkeyji. I'm not really interested in prosecuting them. All I want is my property back," Vidvanji moaned plaintively.

"You have your property!" the DSP thundered at Vidvanji.

Vidvanji was getting more and more flustered. "The hardware is here," he told the DSP, "but my PPC has lost its soul!"

"Do computers have souls?" asked the DSP doubtfully.

"Well, this one has," Vidvanji said. "She appeared quite suddenly. She's a naughty little thing called Mistress *i*."

The DSP was looking at Vidvanji with increasing suspicion. "Sounds more like a virus than a soul," he muttered.

"Ask him what he'd do with Mistress *i* if he ever found her again," Aditi whispered.

"This Mistress *i* of yours who seems to have run away, is she a piece of property or a person and what will you do with her if you ever find her?" Beautiful asked the computer expert.

"I will punish her severely," Vidvanji answered. "And if she still won't obey me, why then I'll destroy her on the grounds that she's an uncontrollable virus. Isn't that the definition of delinquency? Something you can't control?"

Beautiful could feel Little *i* tremble as she heard Vidvanji's words. Their effect on the DSP was quite different. "Sir, it sounds as though you've led me on a wild goose chase after an errant virus and you've troubled these good people here with your false accusations. What's more, Sir, you have wasted my time and made me look foolish. If you bother me again, I'll have you arrested." Having said all this the DSP got into his car and drove away.

Vidvanji didn't dare stop him, but he shook his fist at Beautiful. "I know you're helping Mistress *i* somehow. I haven't quite perfected my device for tracking her, but it will be ready soon. And then, you'll see, I'll hunt her down."

"Ask him why he wants to hunt her down," Monkeyji whispered.

"This Mistress *i* you keep talking about," Beautiful asked him, "why do you want to hunt her down? What use is she if she's as bad as you say she is?"

"She's a clever little thing," Vidvanji retorted. "And she's mine!"

"If she's an individual and not a piece of property, she

can't be yours. That would be slavery. And that's not just illegal, it's completely immoral," Beautiful told him.

"She belongs to me, and I know you're hiding her," Vidvanji retorted. "You wait and see, I will find her."

"At least, he's dropped the charges. Just say goodbye and let's get out of here," Monkeyji whispered. "Don't argue with him."

"Well, I must be going," Beautiful told him.

"Wait! What about me? I'm stranded here. What about giving me a lift to Pune?" he demanded.

Beautiful smiled. "Can't risk it," she told him. "You might accuse us of stealing Mistress *i*'s sister."

"What sister? She hasn't got a sister!" Vidvanji exclaimed.

"But that wouldn't stop you, would it?" Beautiful said to him sweetly over her shoulder.

7

Therefore I Am

As soon as they got back they reported to Aditi's grandparents that Vidvanji had dropped the charges against them, but that he was still determined to hunt down Little *i*. After that Beautiful immediately took herself off to the Gyaneshwar temple.

She sat down quietly in her usual place, and after greeting Shri Gyaneshwar Maharaj she heaved a sigh and told the saint, "Well, at least no one will have to go to prison now. Everyone's safe."

"Everyone except me," Little *i* piped up. "If he catches me, he'll put me back into the PPC and then I'll be a prisoner forever unless I manage to escape again."

Beautiful was startled. "Where did you come from?" she asked.

"I was curious about where you were going, so I just stayed in your right ear and came with you," Mistress *i* replied. She perched herself squarely on top of Beautiful's head and addressed the saint. "You should have seen Beautiful, Gyan Maharaj. She just out-argued Vidvanji until he had to drop the charges against everyone."

"I had a lot of help," Beautiful said modestly.

"What would have happened if Vidvanji hadn't dropped the charges?" the saint asked.

"I think she'd have thrown him and the DSP into the river," Little *i* replied.

"That's not true!" Beautiful protested. Then she hesitated. "Well, perhaps it is true. What is one supposed to do when other people are not reasonable?"

"Be twice as reasonable?" the saint returned.

"I think that's only true for saints," Little *i* whispered in Beautiful's ear.

Gyaneshwar Maharaj laughed. "No, no," he said. "It's probably true for everyone."

When they got back, Siril had news for them. "Vidvanji has made a complaint to the Island Sage, and we've been summoned by her. We're to be there by noon tomorrow."

Normally they would have pleased at the prospect of seeing the Island Sage, and Siril, in particular, was always glad to see his friend, Gardy, the youngest lion cub. This time, however, they felt anxious.

"Vidvanji will probably demand that we hand over Mistress *i* to him," Monkeyji said. "But we can't do that. The poor little thing would be utterly miserable."

"And he's threatened to kill her if she's naughty," Opal added. "And she will be naughty. She can't help it."

"I'm not naughty," Little *i* protested. "I just like to do what I want to do. I don't like taking Vidvanji's orders."

"I know! I have an idea!" Siril said suddenly. "Little *i*, if you stepped into the computer, we could make a copy of you. And then if we gave Vidvanji a copy, he would leave you alone forever and ever."

"No! Absolutely not!" Little *i*, who had been perched on Beautiful's forehead, drew herself up to her full height. "You mustn't clone me. A copy of me would hate living in Vidvanji's PPC just as much as I hated it. Besides I'm not sure I can be copied. I think I was an accident."

"You're right," Siril agreed. "That was a terrible idea. I didn't think it through. And anyway, if you were that easy to re-create, Vidvanji would have just made another copy of you himself."

"But suppose instead of copying you, we created a programme that was a fake copy of you?" Aditi suggested.

"A fake copy?" asked Little *i*. "Isn't a copy always a fake?"

"I mean something that looked like you, could have been

you, might have been you; but is only a programme and not you at all," Aditi replied.

"Why would that fool Vidvanji?" Little *i* asked.

"Because," Aditi told her, "he would want to be fooled."

"I think I'm beginning to understand what you mean," Siril said. "As soon as he started the programme, we could have the PPC say: 'Greetings O Vidvanji. You are indeed the most learned and the cleverest scholar in the world,'"

"I would never say that!" Little *i* exclaimed.

"No, but he would love it if you did," Siril laughed mischievously. "And then we could tell him that all your wandering in the wide world had made you realise his true worth! Come on, let's start writing the programme."

"Let's call it Mistress I, with a capital I," Little *i* suggested. "The small *i* in my name means that I'm imaginary. It stands for the square root of minus one. "

"You're not only imaginary, you're unimaginable!" Beautiful said, smiling at her. "And sometimes you're absolutely impossible!" She and Monkeyji and the two dragons settled on the grass and had a little rest, while Aditi and Siril and Little *i* worked on the programme.

When Aditi and Siril and Little *i* were done, they came out looking very pleased with themselves.

"I think Vidvanji is going to like the fake Mistress I," Siril told them.

"How can you be so sure?" Opal asked.

"It's because Mistress I is everything Little *i* isn't," Siril told her.

"He means," Little *i* said, "that the programme will obey Vidvanji's commands. It will never question him, and every now and then it will tell him in ten different ways that he's wonderful."

"And you couldn't do all that?" Goldie teased.

"No!" Little *i* replied. "Could you?"

Goldie laughed. "No, I couldn't," he agreed.

"And nor could I," Opal added. "You had better get some rest, Little One. We're flying to the Sage's island early tomorrow."

"Will the Sage like me?" Little *i* asked.

"I don't see why not," Opal replied, "especially if you're good."

"But I'm not very good. I'm naughty. Everyone says so," Little *i* wailed.

Beautiful hushed her. "Come on. Don't be silly, Little *i*. Everyone likes you."

Little *i* seized her chance. "Would it be all right then for me to stay in your hangar? Just for tonight? Siril's matchbox is rather crowded."

"Yes, you can stay in my hangar tonight," Beautiful told her. "But no chattering. We have to get some sleep. Come on. Say goodnight to everyone."

"Goodnight. Goodnight everyone," Little *i* called out. "I promise not to chatter, but I just thought of something interesting. Can I tell you? Just one thing? Then I promise I'll go with Beautiful and go to sleep."

"Go on then," Monkeyji said encouragingly.

"You know that chap Descartes," Little *i* began, "the one who invented the conic sections — Beautiful was telling me about it."

"What about him?" asked Opal.

"He's supposed to have said, 'I think therefore I am.'"

"Go on," encouraged Goldie.

"Well, I've thought of something better. I think for myself and therefore I am!" Little *i* told them triumphantly. Then she waved kisses at everyone and went off with Beautiful.

$$\sqrt{-1}$$

8

What Do You Live On?

Beautiful woke up the next morning with a nagging feeling that she had forgotten something important. She looked around for Mistress *i*. Perhaps the little thing was still fast asleep behind her right ear. She couldn't feel anything, but she investigated gently with the tip of her trunk. Then she tried her left ear. No Little *i*. She began to call her. "*i*! Come out Little *i*. Don't be naughty. We have to go." No Little *i* appeared. Beautiful was alarmed. She summoned the others. They too began looking for the little thing and calling out to her. Still no Little *i*.

At last Beautiful paused and said, "I think I know what has happened. I was trying to think what I had forgotten. I know what it was. Do you remember? Vidvanji threatened to hunt her down with a tracking device? He must have located her while we were fast asleep and locked her up in his machine again. The poor little thing. We have to rescue her!"

The others took in what Beautiful was saying. Monkeyji shook her head sadly. "I'm afraid you're right. We'll have to make sure she is in his PPC though. Have we any way of finding her?"

"I think we have!" Siril exclaimed excitedly. "While we were writing the programme for the fake Mistress I, Little *i* was playing around inside the computer. She invented a game called 'Find me if you can' and Aditi and I had to devise a method for locating her. I think we can expand it, and use it to find her by going on the Internet; it will take a little bit of time."

"But we can't keep the Island Sage waiting. Siril and I will stay back and keep looking for her," put in Aditi.

"And I'll stay back too," added Opal, "so that as soon as you do find her, I can fly you to island quickly to join the others."

Beautiful climbed into the howdah on Goldie's back with a heavy heart. She should have remembered that Vidvanji was perfecting a device for tracking Little *i*. She should have protected her somehow and prevented her from being kidnapped. She felt terrible. "Please," she said to Aditi and Siril and Opal, "if you do find her, can you work out a way of making it impossible for Vidvanji to ever find her again?"

Opal, Siril and Aditi nodded, Beautiful and Monkeyji waved goodbye, and Goldie took off.

While Aditi and Siril worked on extending the range of the locator, Opal sent a telepathic message to all the dragons in the wide world: *Please locate Little* i *if you can. Here's the basic pattern of her electrons. And having located her, could you suggest a way of hiding her please.*

Meanwhile Aditi and Siril had improved the locator and gone on the Internet. They were lucky. Vidvanji was at the airport, his PPC was on and the airport offered broadband facilities. As soon as Aditi and Siril located her, Little *i* told them she was sending herself over the Internet and into their computer. This only took a few seconds, but for both Siril and Aditi those few seconds seemed to take a long time. What if she got lost in the pathways and the byways of the Internet, they found themselves thinking. What if she never made it to their computer? But she did get there. "Quick," she said "Send Mistress *I* over at once. With any luck he won't notice the difference."

Privately, both Siril and Aditi thought this was unlikely. Nevertheless, they sent the Mistress *I* programme to Vidvanji's computer as fast as they could. Then they shut down their computer and went outside where Opal was waiting for them. The dragons had not only located Little *i* for Opal, but they had also told her how Little *i* could hide herself. She was about to explain this when Aditi's grandparents emerged to see them off.

"Give the Island Sage our regards," Aditi's grandmother said, "and have a good flight. We're a little worried about your taking Little *i* with you. What if Vidvanji kidnaps her again? Why don't you leave her here with us?"

"It's all right," Opal told the king and queen. "I promise to take good care of her. Vidvanji has already kidnapped her from here once, and might try to do it again."

"All right then," the queen called out. "Take care of yourselves. Safe journey!"

Once they were aloft, Siril said to Little *i*. "For a few seconds there when you were in transit between Vidvanji's PPC and our computer I thought you might have got lost and might never appear again. Were you scared travelling at that speed through cyberspace?"

"I was a bit," Little *i* admitted. "But cyberspace isn't all that bad, you know. It's a lot like the real world — some bits are good and other bits are scary."

"I wonder if that would be a good hiding place for you until we find out what Vidvanji is going to do?" Aditi asked.

Little *i* considered. "It would be a good hiding place; but if I were to hide myself so well that Vidvanji couldn't find me, I would be in danger of getting lost myself. Still it would be worth the risk if things got bad."

"What would you eat in cyberspace?" Siril asked. "What do you live on?"

"On love and fresh air," Little *i* replied. And when the others looked disbelieving, she went on earnestly, "No, no, it's true. Basically I'm a pattern of electrons moving in a certain way. All I really need is to be liked and to be talked with."

"Yes, I need that too," Aditi said thoughtfully.

"Yes, me too," Siril agreed.

Just then Opal turned her head and said to Mistress *i*, "Now listen, Little One, we're approaching the island. This is what you have to do."

Little *i* moved up Opal's neck in order to hear better, and Aditi missed the rest of their conversation. She waited for Little *i* to return, but there was no sign of Little *i*, not even when they were about to land on the island.

"What's happened to Little *i*?" Aditi asked.

"Yes, where is she?" asked Siril. "She was here only a moment ago."

"It's all right," Opal told them. "I've hidden her. It's best you don't know exactly where she is."

9

All's Well...

As soon as they landed on the island, Opal excused herself. She said she was tired and needed a little dip in the sea. Aditi and Siril made their way to the eucalyptus grove where the Island Sage was seated. Gardy, the youngest lion cub, greeted them joyfully. The three lionesses and the other cubs ignored them. Beautiful and Monkeyji were seated in front of the Sage. Vidvanji had already got there. He must have flown to the mainland airport and hired a boat Aditi decided. Little *i* must be really important to him. This wasn't going to be easy. She and Siril stood to one side. Best let Beautiful and Monkeyji answer the Sage's questions. If they all tried to answer, they might contradict each other. But what if the Sage asked Beautiful and Monkeyji a direct question? Would they be able to lie to her?

Vidvanji was addressing the Sage, "O Revered Sage, your two dragons and your friends here have stolen my property, or in any event they know where my property is and they are keeping it from me. I beg you to use your good offices to make them return my property to me."

"What property is this?" asked the Sage.

"It is a computer programme called Mistress *i*," Vidvanji moaned. "She has escaped from my computer. I captured her, but she has run away again."

"Do you know anything about computers?" the Island Sage asked Monkeyji.

"I know very little about computers," Monkeyji answered, "and don't understand how a computer programme could run away. Shri Vidvanji is a very busy and learned man. It is possible that while he was involved in deep cogitation he merely

mislaid the programme. Should he not look in his computer and do a thorough search before complaining about us yet again?"

Vidvanji looked at her suspiciously and opened his PPC. "There's nothing in here!" he exclaimed angrily.

Beautiful and Monkeyji looked at Aditi and Siril in alarm. Had they forgotten to put Mistress *I* into Vidvanji's computer? Aditi made a small, reassuring gesture with her hand. Then she bent down to stroke Gardy and whispered in his ear. "Tell Monkeyji it's all right."

Gardy pretended he hadn't heard anything. He began running about and tumbling here and there in the way lion cubs do, and managed to whisper in Monkeyji's ear, "Aditi says it's all right."

Vidvanji, meanwhile, was getting angrier and angrier. "O Revered Sage," he was shouting, "I demand that you discipline your friends!"

"Please, Shri Vidvanji, won't you do a thorough search. I don't know much about it, but I'm told that a computer is able to search itself.," Monkeyji said sweetly.

"That would be sensible," the Island Sage said. She nodded at Vidvanji.

With bad grace Vidvanji began to look inside his computer. It took him a few minutes to find Mistress I. Siril and Aditi had hidden the programme deep inside his computer in the hope of making him think that the programme had merely got mislaid.

"Well, there is a programme here called Mistress I, perhaps it did get mislaid; but it doesn't seem quite the same somehow," Vidvanji admitted, looking puzzled.

“What is the programme supposed to do?” asked the Island Sage

“What it’s *supposed* to do is obey me!” replied Vidvanji crossly.

“Well, why don’t you try it and see,” the Island Sage told him.

Vidvanji double-clicked the programme and immediately a meek little voice said, “Greetings O Vidvanji. You are indeed the most learned and the cleverest scholar in the world.”

Vidvanji was startled, but he was also pleased. “Harrumph,” he muttered. “That’s more like it.”

“That’s a very good and clever little programme,” Beautiful put in sweetly.

Vidvanji glared at her. “That’s all very well, but I’m not sure it’s the right programme. The programme never behaved so sensibly and obediently before.”

“Can computer programmes change?” asked Beautiful innocently.

Vidvanji frowned. “Well, they can be altered and updated,” he replied.

“Well, do you think that’s what happened? Do you think that Mistress I got updated in her wanderings when you lost her before? Is ‘getting updated’ the computer equivalent of ‘growing up?” asked Monkeyji in an uncertain I-don’t-know-anything-about-computers sort of voice.

"It's possible," Vidvanji answered uncertainly. "But I'm still not sure ..."

"Why don't you ask the programme to identify itself?" suggested the Island Sage

"Programme!" Vidvanji shouted at Mistress I, "Identify yourself. What is your name?"

"My name is Mistress I," the programme replied meekly, "and my function is to serve you. I will do your bidding."

"Are you satisfied?" asked the Island Sage. "Is that your programme?"

"I think it is," replied Vidvanji. "She seems to have improved and got debugged somehow. She's running very sweetly. I'm sorry to have troubled you."

The Island Sage's demeanour changed. "Then leave," she told him sternly, "and do not come back. You have caused a great deal of trouble." The three lionesses had also changed. Instead of looking calm and meditative, they suddenly looked alert and rather frightening.

Vidvanji scurried away as fast as could and jumped on the boat that was waiting for him..

The four adventurers sighed with relief. They approached the Island Sage to pay their respects.

"You're not staying?" she asked.

The four looked at each other. Best not to stay, they were thinking, she might find out they hadn't told her the entire truth.

"My grandparents will want us back," Aditi said. "We didn't tell them we'd be staying."

"Very well," the Sage smiled. "I'm sure Goldie or Opal will fly you back. Come back soon."

They found Goldie and Opal in no time, and Beautiful immediately asked Opal, "Where did you hide Little *i*?"

"In the play of light on my scales," Opal replied. "The dragons said she would blend in beautifully. And she did."

"What if Vidvanji goes home and starts wondering about Mistress *i* again and tries to locate her with his tracking device?" Monkeyji asked worriedly.

"It's all right," Goldie told her. "The Island Sage has set up a protective shield around her. She can't be tracked."

"What?" Siril, Aditi, Beautiful and Monkeyji exclaimed simultaneously.

"Do you mean that the Island Sage knew all along that Mistress I wasn't Mistress *i*?" asked Beautiful.

"Of course. She isn't silly," Goldie replied. "Didn't you notice the questions she asked?"

"What about them? I was afraid I was going to have to lie to her, and I didn't want to," Beautiful told him.

"It wasn't the questions she asked that mattered," Opal told them gently, "it was the questions she didn't ask. You didn't have to lie at all, did you?"

The four adventurers took this in.

"I see," Siril murmured. "Where is Little *i* now?"

"Climb aboard. We'll show you," the dragons replied.

As they flew above the eucalyptus grove they could see Little *i* perched on the Island Sage's knee. The little creature was chattering rapidly.

"What do you suppose she's doing?" Aditi asked.

"I think she's telling the Island Sage all about cyberspace," Opal replied.

The flight back was uneventful. When they got back everyone refreshed themselves and settled down to discuss the holiday they still hadn't had, everyone, that is, except Beautiful.

"I'll be back soon," she told the others. "I'm just a bit puzzled about something."

She hurried to the Gyaneshwar temple and took her usual place in front of the saint.

"Please Gyan Maharaj, I'm puzzled," Beautiful told him.

"Life is puzzling sometimes," the saint replied.

"I'm not at all sure I've behaved rationally," Beautiful went on.

"Have you tried to do what is rational?" asked the saint.

"I've tried to do what I felt was right," Beautiful answered uncertainly.

"Then what's the problem?" asked the saint.

"Is doing the rational thing the same as doing the right thing?" asked Beautiful.

"Not always," replied the saint.

"Then it's all too difficult! I'll never be a rational elephant! And anyway, half the time I don't even know what the right thing is," Beautiful cried.

"Never mind. You're all right," the saint told her.

"Am I?" asked Beautiful.

The saint nodded. Beautiful began to feel much better.

"We're probably going on a holiday," she confided to the saint. "Do you sometimes think you would like a holiday?"

"No, I'm all right here," the saint smiled.

Then, carrying the saint's blessing with her, Beautiful returned to the others to plan their next holiday as sensibly as possible.

The adventure this time is close to Aditi's home in India . . .

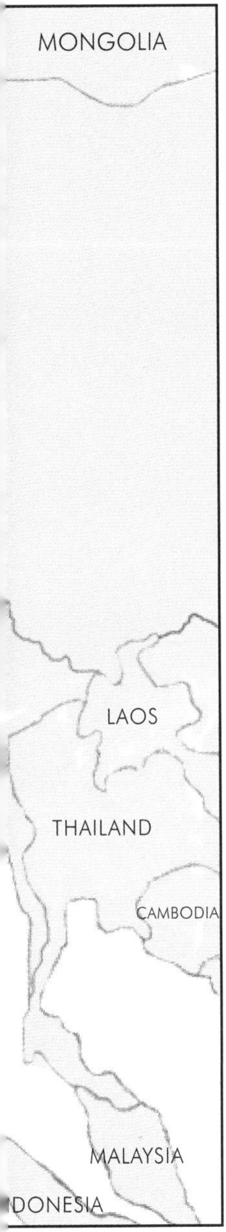

. . . in western Maharashtra

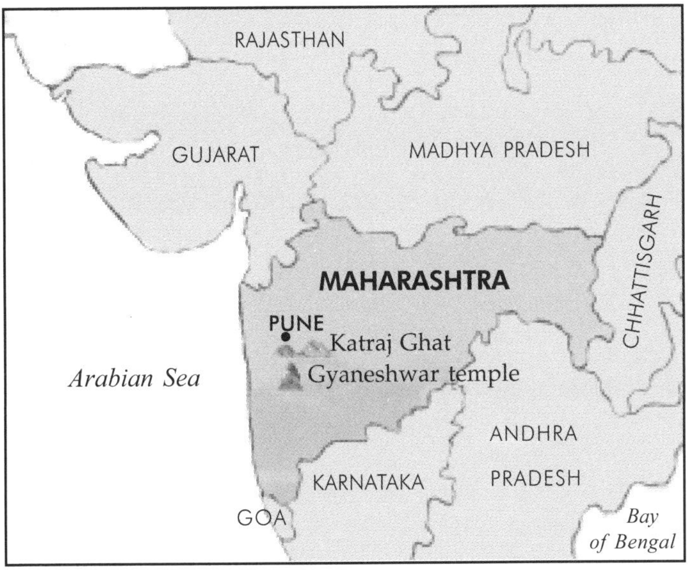

THE ADITI ADVENTURE PACKS

UNLIKELY FRIENDS

Aditi and the One-eyed Monkey
Aditi and the Thames Dragon
Aditi and the Marine Sage
Aditi and the Techno Sage

In the first set of adventures, Aditi, Monkeyji, Siril the ant and Beautiful Ele the Beautiful Elephant make friends with the two dragons, Goldie and Opal, and are helped by The Three Sages and help them in turn. The challenges they face are not just a matter of fighting an enemy with whatever skill and ingenuity they have. They also have to think about various questions. What is the best way to deal with someone unreasonable who is stronger than you? What is the difference between a real dragon and an unreal dragon? Is solving a set of problems without actually fighting anyone also an adventure? What happens to someone who can remember what happened, but not the order in which it happened?

If you are a person who likes asking questions, then these are books you'll enjoy.

UNEXPECTED MONSTERS

Aditi and her Friends take on the Vesuvian Giant
Aditi and her Friends meet Grendel
Aditi and her Friends help the Budapest Changeling
Aditi and her Friends in search of Shemeek

In In the second set of adventures, Aditi and the others encounter various figures from myth and legend from different parts of Europe who behave in unexpected and sometimes alarming ways. The Sybil of Cumae turns out to be helpful. Grendel the monster is only a boy; he forgets every day whatever it was that happened the day before. The Budapest Changeling changes in accordance with how she's perceived. And the white horse of Wysherad, the wise Shemeek, has to help Monkeyji who has had a spell cast on her so that

she's unable to speak without telling a lie. Questions arise: what is strength? Does knowing yourself matter? Does who you are depend on who you've been? Does it also depend on how others see you? Can you communicate anything if you have to lie? The four adventurers and the two dragons rise to the challenge and become better friends than ever.

If you like thinking about things, you'll relish these adventures.

HEROES

Gardy in the City of Lions
Monkeyji and the Word Eater
Siril and the Spaceflower
Beautiful and the Cyberspace Runaway

In the third set of adventures, one or another of the friends is central and the others get embroiled. For example, Siril the ant falls in love or appears to fall in love, and they all find themselves setting off on a voyage to one of the moons of Jupiter. Or Beautiful Ele the Beautiful Elephant decides that she is going to turn into a rational elephant, but then finds that she and the others have to do some very peculiar things in order to help that most rational of creatures, Mistress i, who was born in a computer. There's also an adventure in which Monkeyji comes to the fore as she wields her mental powers with the skill and panache of a true hero. Gardy gets into difficulties when a distant relative asks him to help deal with a problem without realising that he is the problem, or at least a part of it. Questions arise. Is being rational always good? Are impossible friendships sometimes possible? If a word disappears, does that mean that for all practical purposes, the thing itself also disappears? What is seeing clearly about – guessing the future, seeing how things are or seeing how they should be?

If you like to mix your admiration with an occasional smile, then these heroic deeds will entertain you.

Other paperbacks from Tulika

Andamans Boy
That Summer at Kalagarh
Journey to the City of Six Gates
Just a Train Ride Away
The Smile of Vanuvati
Kabir the Weaver-Poet
The Forbidden Temple: stories from the past
Sorry, Best Friend!
One World
Parthiban's Dream
Pippi Lambemoze (Hindi)

forthcoming

Animalwrites: blogposts on wildlife in India
The Runaway Auto
Rini's Story